Customer Service Skills for Managers

Customer Service Skills for Managers

Series " Management Skills for Managers "
By: D.K. Hawkins
Version 1.1 ~September 2021
Published by D.K. Hawkins at KDP
Copyright ©2021 by D.K. Hawkins. All rights reserved.

No part of this publication may be reproduced, distributed or transmitted in any form or by any means including photocopying, recording or other electronic or mechanical methods or by any information storage or retrieval system without the prior written permission of the publishers, except in the case of very brief quotations embodied in critical reviews and certain other noncommercial uses permitted by copyright law.

All rights reserved, including the right of reproduction in whole or in part in any form.

All information in this book has been carefully researched and checked for factual accuracy. However, the author and publisher make no warranty, express or implied, that the information contained herein is appropriate for every individual, situation, or purpose and assume no responsibility for errors or omissions.

The reader assumes the risk and full responsibility for all actions. The author will not be held responsible for any loss or damage, whether consequential, incidental, special, or otherwise, that may result from the information presented in this book.

All images are free for use or purchased from stock photo sites or royalty-free for commercial use. I have relied on my own observations as well as many different sources for this book, and I have done my best to check facts and give credit where it is due. In the event that any material is used without proper permission, please contact me so that the oversight can be corrected

The information provided in this book is for informational purposes only and is not intended to be a source of advice or credit analysis with respect to the material presented. The information and/or documents contained in this book do not constitute legal or financial advice and should never be used without first consulting with a financial professional to determine what may be best for your individual needs.

The publisher and the author do not make any guarantee or other promise as to any results that may be obtained from using the content of this book. You should never make any investment decision without first consulting with your own financial advisor and conducting your own research and due diligence. To the maximum extent permitted by law, the publisher and the author disclaim any and all liability in the event any information, commentary, analysis, opinions, advice and/or recommendations contained in this book prove to be inaccurate, incomplete or unreliable, or result in any investment or other losses.

Content contained or made available through this book is not intended to and does not constitute legal advice or investment advice and no attorney-client relationship is formed. The publisher and the author are providing this book and its contents on an "as is" basis. Your use of the information in this book is at your own risk.

TABLE OF CONTENTS.

TABLE OF CONTENTS. 4

INTRODUCTION. 6

CHAPTER 1 8

    Customer Service Development For Managers' Personal Growth. 8

CHAPTER 2 15

    Are You Handling Customers Or Managing Traumas in Customer Service? 15

CHAPTER 3 23

    Important Components Of Outstanding Customer Service You Must Know. 23

CHAPTER 4 28

    How to Communicate Your Superior Customer Service Ability to Your Customers. 28

CHAPTER 5 32

    Customer Service Competencies And Its Important Moments For Excellence. 32

CHAPTER 6 37

    What a Manager Can Do to Change Poor Customer Service. 37

CHAPTER 7 42

    How to Resolve Complaints About Customer Service. 42

CHAPTER 8 46

The Manager's Contribution to the Development of a Customer Service Culture. 46

CHAPTER 9 52

The Crucial Steps to Exceptional Customer Service. 52

CHAPTER 10 58

Customer Service and Developing a Culture of High Performance. 58

CHAPTER 11 64

Overnight Improvement of Your Customer Service Skills 64

CONCLUSION. 71

INTRODUCTION.

Successful managers recognize the importance of providing an outstanding client experience. To run a business that relies on "new" customers is costly. By providing excellent and consistent customer service, you can turn customers into repeat and loyal customers.

Making a customer feel welcome and valued requires knowing how to deal with a complaint, greet a customer, and making a customer feel appreciated. A company's bottom line benefits when employees understand and consistently provide this level of service at all times.

Often, these are the most challenging talents to acquire in the job but impact customer service and management objectives. Managers have a unique chance to instill this important skill set in their teams by demonstrating and demonstrating these important customer service traits themselves.

When managers have effective customer service skills, they provide real reinforcement for their sales and marketing infrastructure and empower important personnel who contribute significantly to its long-term success.

Customer service is important, and no one can convince you otherwise. I've been utilizing these customer service techniques discussed in this BOOK for the last decade, and I'm here to tell you that they work. Customers will begin to recognize you by name and approach you to say hello whenever they enter your shop or organization.

Consider reworking your customer service approach as a manager if you want to increase your sales and profitability. If something isn't right, correct it immediately. This is an excellent method for implementing improvements in your organization - keep this in mind. Are you ready to develop or hone your customer service skills? If yes, then let's get started.

CHAPTER 1

Customer Service Development For Managers' Personal Growth.

A job is important for a person's development, not just for his requirements but also for his personal growth, and acquiring customer service skills will aid in this personal growth. While the job may not be easy, it may also be quite rewarding.

Customer service jobs that were previously mostly outsourced are beginning to return, which is good news for those interested in entering this field. Individuals who enter this field of work will also have many prospects for advancement and possibly future managerial roles in the sector.

While many businesses previously placed a low premium on customer assistance due to the lack of face-to-face interaction with clients via the internet, this is no longer the case. Shipments were made, and consumer complaints were not given proper consideration, as with customer service.

However, as a result of competition, a complete turnaround has occurred, and effective customer service skills are now widely employed, yielding positive outcomes for businesses that practice them. Customers who receive the information they seek while also seeing that their problems are addressed will always return.

Companies nowadays want all their consumers to be satisfied and contented. Therefore, improving customer support service is always a top priority. There are also courses available nowadays that teach people how to improve their customer service skills; these are courses that may be delivered to the workforce of a particular firm.

This can take the shape of seminars, as customer service training does not have to be official. If seminars are conducted intensively, participants will have a decent opportunity of gaining valuable knowledge.

Individuals can acquire customer service abilities in their first employment. This is to comprehend the wants of clients by placing oneself in their shoes. This can only be plain sense, which a person will readily understand. However, not everyone will immediately get this; many wills. While some will want additional time to comprehend it fully, others will take it in stride.

While some individuals learn and comprehend the value of customer assistance and its benefits for their particular careers, they may lack the motivation to strive for more. Excellent customer service can pave the way for personal growth in your profession. This might be your path to future growth and perhaps management jobs.

This is possible even without formal training in the customer support service line. Your excellent performance as an employee and your role in providing excellent customer service will serve as a foundation for growth and advancement.

In any business, excellent customer service lays the groundwork for client pleasure. However, delighted consumers benefit more than just sales; they benefit everyone. Both sales workers and customer service telephone agents can gain from satisfied consumers.

Everyone has visited a store or business where an employee went above and beyond what was requested. You may have had an excellent server who never left your drink alone, or a salesperson may have returned immediately with a different size pair of trousers. Everyone has had an employee aid them, and they needed to inform the manager of their accomplishments.

Going above and above the bare minimum job requirements will set you apart in any professional situation. Ensuring that each customer you assist is as satisfied as possible helps you appear an excellent employee. This is incredibly satisfying when a customer expresses an opinion or when management observes the extra effort you put into your job.

You should not be afraid to ask management about possible customer service training if you need help in this area. The chances are that a DVD on customer service or other training materials for employees will provide you with the tools you need to meet and exceed consumer expectations.

Everybody works for money, and the more money you earn, the better off you are. So, what is the best approach to increase your earnings?

Pursue a promotion. Positivity and exceeding job standards are the best ways to get started on the path to promotion.

Many employees desire advancement but have no idea how to obtain one, let alone become noticed employees. Unfortunately, there is no foolproof strategy for success, as the world is constantly changing. However, the only surefire strategy to increase your visibility in the workplace is to be an exceptional customer service representative and hone your customer service skills.

Nobody relishes the prospect of interacting with a moody sales assistant. Whether the grin is genuine or artificial, a smile and a cheerful individual make clients feel more welcome. Conversely, speaking with a customer in a "chipper" and "happy-to-be-at-work" tone will urge them to return and ask you any additional questions.

Knowledge of the products you sell or comprehensive knowledge of the organization you work for will make responding to queries easier. It will also demonstrate to your bosses that you care.

If a consumer contacts you with a question, it does not help your promotion efforts if you are forced to refer them to another employee. You could also send the promotion to the other colleague, which does not appear suitable in the eyes of customers or management.

Creating a welcome experience for your consumer can help you stand out from associates who do not prioritize customer satisfaction. Being known for going above the tasks assigned to you by your superiors can earn you a favorable reputation, resulting in a faster promotion.

Employers hire and work to keep employees who contribute to the success of their organization, correct? Therefore, go the extra mile to gratify the customer and position yourself for success.

Enrolling in vocational classes that teach customer service abilities can also help develop customer service skills. This can be accomplished in your spare time while also establishing and strengthening your professional record, benefiting your personal development and advancement.

You can earn good credentials through the occupational courses you take and the seminars and training you attend. All these factors will increase your prospects of advancement and the possibility of obtaining management roles, albeit this may not be easy due to the high demand for these positions.

However, your customer service abilities will come in handy.

CHAPTER 2

Are You Handling Customers Or Managing Traumas in Customer Service?

Customer support quarterly audits should encompass all aspects of customer service, from the moment a customer enters the showroom to service and parts to post-sales assistance and marketing. In essence, managers must question themselves, "Are we prioritizing our clients, our most valuable asset?"

These examinations should be thorough but not complicated and should generally follow these six procedures.

Step One: Are client handling methods and customer service excellence ingrained in the organizational culture?

From the lowest management level to the highest, each employee must view customer service as an intrinsic aspect of their job.

In the future, customer service will be as routine as breathing, using a cell phone, or grabbing a cup of coffee every morning. It's unnecessary to go overboard to make an excellent first impression, and frequently, it's the little things that stick with clients. Think of it like this:

- A timely return of a phone call

- A sincere, pleasant greeting or smile

- A card to commemorate a wondrous occasion, such as the anniversary of the purchase of an automobile.

- A letter of appreciation

- Each employee greets each other with a pleasant greeting during each interaction

Every employee must go above and beyond to ensure that each customer feels welcome. Whether on the phone, in person, or online, even if the customer collaborates with another employee.

As part of the customer service process, ensure that correct, standardized data is collected and documented for each customer. Utilize automated systems to schedule times, kinds, and dates for follow-up and ensure that processes are followed.

Step Two: Are we replying to each consumer promptly and personally?

Managers, sales teams, and service workers can respond to each consumer immediately and individually. Each employee should place themselves in their clients' shoes, visualize how they would like to be treated, and behave accordingly.

Are the sales representatives contacting customers to ascertain their level of satisfaction with the deals?

Has the service department contacted you to schedule an appointment?

Proactive customer service is just as important as responding to their issues and inquiries. Examine existing processes that have been built to capture each encounter to respond to future client inquiries efficiently and with accurate information.

Disconnect the automatic response on the Internet - each request should be individualized and responded to by a human from the dealer, not a machine. Managers should validate this system by sending an inquiry using an email account not associated with the dealer.

Step Three: Do we proactively communicate with our customers?

Maintaining customers and utilizing them as references requires effective communication. It is vital to keep customers informed about the status of their vehicles, whether they are new cars ordered from another dealer or the factory or vehicles that are being serviced or updated.

Customer service protocols should explicitly identify what to do in the event of a change that could affect customer satisfaction. If a customer's automobile will be delayed, notify them as soon as possible and inform them honestly about the situation. If a customer is promised a car by a specific date and delays, inform them immediately and honestly about when you expect the issue to be handled.

Are newsletter distribution systems automated to give dealer and manufacturer updates, news, and other information?

Is customer data utilized to prospect based on family milestones that may necessitate the purchase of a car (a child's approaching sixteenth birthday or graduation)?

Step Four: Are we praising our consumers visibly and continuously?

Customer handling operations should demonstrate a sense of welcome and appreciation for customers from the moment they are greeted throughout their experience, including post-sales and servicing. Verify that protocols define how to collect their data, ascertain their needs and connect them with an associate who can assist them in purchasing the car or services they desire.

Are consumers who visit the dealer or service department greeted with a sense of welcome?

Are basic amenities such as coffee, water, and a comfortable seating space provided?

Do we keep a basket of toys on hand if children accompany their parents?

Fewer distractions result in a more enjoyable experience, which results in more sales. Most importantly, do we express gratitude to the consumer for their visit, interest, time, and purchase?

Step Five: Do we solicit and act on client feedback?

Examine the mechanisms in place to collect client feedback.

Are we sending them pre-addressed response cards or an e-mail survey requesting their feedback on their experience?

How often is their input sought?

What becomes of the feedback that is received?

Adapt customer service operations to meet better the needs of all customers based on direct feedback and express gratitude to consumers who assist you in making a difference.

Are customer appreciation events such as workshops and VIP screenings planned?

Is data from these incidents being collected and analyzed to provide more feedback?

Step Six: Are we constantly experimenting with new approaches to provide superior service?

While customer service is the duty of every employee, it begins with the dealer. Managers are accountable for teaching superior customer service abilities, but they must also model these behaviors for their staff as leaders. Customer service excellence requires the knowledge that the primary responsibility is to assist people in selecting the correct automobile, not to sell vehicles.

Quarterly customer care check-ups allow managers to analyze their client service and customer handling processes and determine whether these processes are being followed consistently. Instead of dealing with customer catastrophes, managers may use this data to make rational judgments about improving the customer experience.

CHAPTER 3

Important Components Of Outstanding Customer Service You Must Know.

What factors contribute to an exceptional, rewarding customer service experience? If you're a customer, it's the smile on your face following a painless transaction and the goal to purchase from that firm many times.

From a business's standpoint, it's a synthesis of many important factors. Learn the principles of excellent customer service below to help you earn repeat business and attract new customers.

To ensure seamless transactions, utilize a reputable software/tool that enables you to collect important customer information such as contact information, product/service preferences, purchase history, and payment methods. The system must be readily available to all employees to facilitate data management.

Naturally, your team must be thoroughly trained to operate the system.

Proactive problem resolution - A proactive, forward-thinking customer care team works to anticipate and resolve potential problems. It's simple to be proactive. Inquire about your client's likes and dislikes regarding your products and/or services.

Allow them to illuminate what they wish to modify or improve. This enables your organization to quickly identify areas of consumer unhappiness and develop a strategy to address them effectively.

Ongoing training and development - Another important component of providing good customer service is doing frequent staff training. Apart from the fact that staff requires refresher training regularly, training also assists them in honing their customer service skills.

Also, products and equipment and customer service methodologies are constantly evolving. Training will keep your employees informed of market developments and, eventually, new ways to delight your customers.

Friendliness and helpfulness - Friendliness and helpfulness can be demonstrated in person, over the phone, or even online. However, this is especially true and visible for staff who work directly with customers.

Remember that a simple grin and hello might make an impression on a consumer. Assist clients as best you can with their orders, inquiries, and difficulties. Assure them that you are more than willing to assist them with their needs.

Timeliness refers to consistently satisfying consumers' demands for delivery, response times, and order fulfillment. As a customer-focused organization, you aim to minimize wait times. Customers are not the most forgiving individuals, so establish a fair timeframe and adhere to it. Advise clients if there may be delays and keep them informed of the status.

Product and/or service quality - Your customers place a premium on the quality of your offerings. It's fantastic to have the best products/services on the market. That is not always the case, however.

Occasionally, clients are looking for an acceptable product or service since they are on a budget. As such, ensure that the product or service you give meets the expectations of your target market.

While this may seem small, it is an important aspect of providing excellent customer service. The environment can take the shape of a brick-and-mortar store or an internet store.

Is your store neat and orderly?

Is your website intuitive and well-designed?

Consider these seemingly insignificant details since they have a significant impact on your consumers and prospects.

To properly cultivate a customer service culture inside your organization, each staff member should be familiar with and understand five important components of outstanding customer service. When these are carried out successfully, your firm will undoubtedly benefit from retaining existing customers and gaining new ones.

CHAPTER 4

How to Communicate Your Superior Customer Service Ability to Your Customers.

This is an often asked question by customer service managers or reps. They merely want to reassure clients that they have nothing to fear because they know how to provide them with what they desire, but they cannot do so respectfully.

It is merely disrespectful to inform consumers that "I am an expert or I am knowledgeable about what I do" or "relax, sir; I know my work." Often, even with more than a decade of expertise in customer service, encounter this issue. The straightforward remedy is to let them know that you are ready to go as a fantastic customer service manager or representative.

Avoid disappointment.

Customer service representatives, and I mean genuinely excellent and experienced representatives, often report that they have been informed, "you are not as experienced, you are not up to par, or you are not the greatest at what you do." It's the awkward moment when you must maintain your composure and refrain from being disappointed.

They assert this because they have no concept of being the best at one's work. It is not the outcome that determines the best. Other than that, it is your concern and concern for the outcome that makes you the best. As a result, you must maintain your composure and avoid disappointment.

While I recognize you as an expert, there is always space for improvement. Take the statement in stride; instead, use it as an opportunity to develop yourself. Not by responding but by just continuing to do your job, you can demonstrate that you are an expert by giving excellent customer service.

Instead of bullying, show appreciation.

Demonstrate to your customers what they desire. Concentrate on their needs rather than bullying their opinions and interpreting them negatively. Rather than becoming irritated by their words and unpleasant approaches, be helpful. This will undoubtedly demonstrate your abilities to your clientele.

Above all, Accept.

If you fail to provide them (customers) with what they desire or require, they will undoubtedly complain to your manager or higher authority; it's that simple and impolite. When something happens that should not happen, accept it gently.

Be proactive rather than reactive. Avoid expressing angry or blaming the consumer; accept it and strive to improve. Again, there is room for improvement when it comes to providing exceptional customer service.

Not easy, is it? To be honest, nothing is ever that simple. Always remember that you gain by working. You converse, and you lose. Therefore, refrain from speaking back; perform your work, and your consumers will understand that you are experienced and truly the greatest at what you do; you won't have to tell them that. We're delighted to provide superior client service.

Providing excellent customer service enables a business to retain existing customers and attract new ones. Thus, superior customer service enables a business to thrive and prosper.

CHAPTER 5

Customer Service Competencies And Its Important Moments For Excellence.

A customer support superstar is empathetic, pleasant, and helpful. Are you paying attention? Listening is the pinnacle of their courtesy. The quality of the client engagement is the linchpin of outstanding customer service.

This requires you to treat consumers with dignity, respect, and consideration. Customer loyalty is eroded by poor personnel attitudes and a lack of respect. Duh? It is only logical.

Do you hear this correctly?

Consider the following two strategies for working with people and consumers. The first is a self-centered approach to interpersonal relationships. This indicates that your primary emphasis is on yourself and not on others.

What matters most is what is happening to you, how it impacts you, and why you dislike or enjoy it. If anything does not go your way, you become agitated, frustrated, and furious and communicate your feelings to others. This is the incorrect method of customer service. It is caused by a lack of maturity or a callous attitude. Carelessness is an illness that must be healed.

The alternative approach is other-centered. Your objective here is to assist others, specifically consumers or coworkers. 'Help other people get what they want, and you will get what you want,' remarked Bob Conklin, a highly successful and respected businessman. Take note of how he stated this. You first assist, and you receive.

When done honestly and with integrity, this is a caring approach. In other words, you are concerned with the consequences of your actions. You wish them well and do your best to help them. This is a prerequisite for superstars of customer service.

Your client engagement can be classified into four categories. The following are the definitions:

Moment of Truth; any action you take that directly impacts how clients perceive you (remember, you are the company you work for) or your organization.

Moment of Disappointment; when you fall short of the customer's expectations. This is a substandard service.

Moment of Inadequate Performance; when you only satisfy a customer's expectation. This is a standard level of service.

The Moment of Magic occurs when you exceed a customer's expectation. This is an instance of superior customer service.

The purpose of a customer service superstar is to treat consumers far better than they expect by self-managing each important moment of truth to ensure the customer receives excellent service. Consider what impresses you as a customer to determine what to do. Also, consider what you hope customer support representatives would accomplish.

All exceptional service begins with deference and kindness. Following that, the service provider must be engaging and optimistic. This may entail asking a few questions and paying attention to the customer's goals or needs. The service provider must immediately begin resolving the customer's issue.

This may include clarifying the product or service, providing alternatives, resolving a worry or issue, or just taking an order. A successful conclusion to serving the customer involves a summary, concluding positive comments, and a thank you. The finest service providers are constantly on the lookout for ways to provide value.

You accomplish all of this inside the area of our job's important moments. It is a science in the sense that particular procedures must be followed. It's an art form because you infuse it with your individuality and flair while treating each consumer as an individual. This is the essence of a rockstar in customer service.

CHAPTER 6

What a Manager Can Do to Change Poor Customer Service.

Whose Fault Is It Anyway?

Stand at any check-out line and see the bleak face. Call your service provider and listen to the voice of disinterest. In the workplace, deception, abuse, mistrust, disorganization, lying, and cheating are widespread. Businesses and departments are plagued with negativity, sucking the vitality out of individuals tasked with "loving on their consumers."

Many of us wonder why people aren't more enthusiastic about their professions in an age of scarcity. As CEOs and managers, we must set a positive example and infuse our customer service professionals with positive energy for the client and one another.

To find out whether there is an underlying issue that has not been addressed, executives, managers, and supervisors must ask some challenging questions.

"Do what I say, not what I do."

Observing the boss make exceptions to the rules for himself/herself and chosen favorites questions any standards the organization may be attempting to establish. Also, it confuses the team on the expectations and penalties.

Employees will only do what is necessary to ensure their survival or the organization's survival as a whole. This will lead to apathy. There will be a shortage of caring employees in the future, making it impossible to provide outstanding customer service.

Consider the following:

1) Do I ever use profanity?

2) Do I refer to my staff or customers as morons, stupid, useless, or any other derogatory terms?

3) Do I differentiate between internal and external customers?

4) Do I make a point of expressing my gratitude and appreciation?

5) Am I smiling?

6) Do I maintain eye contact with individuals?

If you haven't worked out that your responses to questions 1-3 should be negative and your responses to questions 4-6 should be affirmative, it's reasonable to assume that you are not leading by example.

The good news is that these six questions can be turned into action plans for you personally. The more you change yourself, the more you transform your organization or department.

"I'm assuming you're aware."

As a consultant, I often hear managers extol the virtues of their customer service team. Also, customer service employees will state that they are trying their best. However, while listening to actual customer interactions, an evident communication or service gap often emerges. The tools they lack may be technological or informational, but more often than not, they lack what our grandmothers referred to as "social graces."

Social Graces are a set of abilities that enable someone to communicate politely in social situations. They include deportment, etiquette, behavior, and fashion. As managers, we take for granted that everyone understands, if not agrees, that social graces are also business standards.

To our amazement, we now have an entire generation of professionals that prefer virtual worlds or texting to face-to-face engagement! These employees may be oblivious of their lack of professional etiquette, which directly affects their impression of your consumers.

What can a manager do to prevent falling into the trap of making broad assumptions?

1) Conduct a work analysis for the department to see which tools or abilities are lacking.

2) Establish a mentorship program. Utilize your in-house talent to educate and serve as a sounding board for some of the more complicated human interactions that occur. This can be a significant benefit to a new hire or young employee.

3) Incorporate a third-party Secret Shopper or call monitoring program that is helpful at flushing out flaws. Often, the purpose of these programs is to concentrate exclusively on the positive aspects of the customer service representative's performance.

CHAPTER 7

How to Resolve Complaints About Customer Service.

Regardless of your perspective, customer service is an important component of every organization, much more so during difficult economic times. Customer service is much more than functioning as the customer's point of contact. When carried out properly by skilled personnel, it can significantly boost earnings, client loyalty, and retention.

One important area is what is referred to as active listening. This includes behavior that reflects a company's alignment with its customers.

While we all desire to be heard, a skilled customer service person can subdue this desire. Rather than spending time formulating their thoughts and determining the most effective way to communicate their opinions, they actively listen.

This means they can listen attentively while making appropriate noises and inserting words into the conversation to demonstrate that they are following the customer's train of thought.

How to Resolve Complaints in Seven Easy Steps.

To deal with complaints efficiently, you must exhibit your abilities and your ability to handle issues. To accomplish this, follow these seven steps.

Step 1; Begin by honestly and unequivocally apologizing. Inform the customer that you accept responsibility and plan to assist him or her in determining an acceptable solution. The sooner you demonstrate to the customer that you are on their side, the better.

Step 2: Active listening is important. Ask as many inquiries as possible to elicit as much information as possible while also demonstrating to the consumer that you are interested in their problem. Active listening requires you to make positive sounds to demonstrate that you are paying attention. Avoid interfering at all costs.

Step 3: Active listeners often repeat key messages received back to the client or other individual they interact with to ensure that the key points have been grasped. While this does not require you to agree on everything, it does provide a framework for minimizing misunderstandings.

Step 4: Determine the customer's desires. Often, they are unsure of what they desire. Indeed, they may be looking for an outlet for their displeasure. Avoid the error of seeking a solution too soon; instead, listen to them out.

Step 5: Always demonstrate empathy for the customer. This demonstrates that you share their feelings and that you genuinely want to fix the situation.

Never take a defensive position. If you're truly skilled, you may be able to soothe someone by matching their tone and tempo. A good course of action is to keep your cool at all times, even if caution is advised, because this could be interpreted as anger towards your customer.

Step 6: You may need to conduct additional research but agree on a timetable first, even if you cannot settle the situation immediately. Ascertain that you understand what you agreed to do and that you phone back when you said you would, even if it is only to inform you that the issue would take longer to handle than you anticipated.

Step 7: If possible, direct concerns to a customer service department or manager who will take responsibility; this will enable you to take preventative measures to avoid recurrences. Once the issue has been rectified, consider whether you can genuinely exceed the customer's expectations. A properly handled complaint might increase consumer loyalty.

CHAPTER 8

The Manager's Contribution to the Development of a Customer Service Culture.

As a manager, you can take three important measures to create, promote, and sustain an organizational customer service culture.

Do your personnel merely serve clients, or do they genuinely care about assisting them in resolving their issues?

Do they understand that each interaction with their internal or external consumers is a watershed moment?

Do they realize that their encounter will influence whether the consumer perceives your organization as helpful, kind, approachable, or cold, uninterested, and unwelcome?

1. Create a customer service mission statement. This process begins with determining the substantial influence of your organization's services on both internal and external clients.

Consider the advantages that your product or service provides to your customers in addition to the obvious qualities. For instance, an anti-lock braking system manufacturer does more than creating a product. Their product, in the end, will save lives.

Following that, describe the picture you wish to convey to your customers. For instance, a call center's mission statement might read as follows: "To take responsibility for each call, to manage each request appropriately, to dispatch efficiently and to communicate effectively to achieve the customer's complete happiness."

As another example, J.B. Hunt Transportation's goal statement is "Providing the best service and solutions to maximize customer productivity and happiness."

Finally, devise a method for bringing this image to life. This will include the following two steps: ensuring that both personnel and organizational processes are customer-focused.

2. Instill a customer service mindset and focus on your personnel. Each employee's engagement with customers must support the customer service purpose.

Examine the "moments of truth" during which your clients interact with your business. You want your employees to be glad and responsive during these moments consistently.

Remember that customer service is a shared obligation shared by all employees. It is not restricted to individuals who work at the front desk or service desk. It is impossible to foresee when a customer may contact your firm.

Stress and emphasize the important customer service characteristics and abilities required to fulfill your organization's customer service purpose. For instance, the first point of contact for potential clients is often a receptionist.

This individual must be friendly, approachable, hospitable, and helpful. Employees responsible for resolving client concerns must possess strong listening, communication, and problem-solving abilities.

When recruiting new staff, emphasize customer service; when screening applications, incorporate behavioral interviews to question how they handle various customer service scenarios. After hiring the team, develop qualitative and quantitative performance standards and metrics to verify that the appropriate customer care abilities are used during client interactions.

3. Ensure that organizational systems, rules, and procedures support the customer service mission. Put your workers in the uncomfortable situation of possessing the desire and ability to offer exceptional

customer service but lacking the systems or procedures necessary to carry it out.

Empower staffs that are closest to the client's situation to make important decisions on resolution. Recognize and address inconsistencies in performance objectives. For example, avoid placing staff in a Catch-22 situation where they are expected to satisfy customers while also being evaluated based on the number of customers serviced in a specific period.

Ascertain that when one department commits to a customer, the other departments can keep that commitment. Create incentive schemes to reward customers who provide superior service. Conduct consumer surveys and, where possible, act on their responses.

Verify that workers have the necessary training and tools to deliver the appropriate level of customer care. Give them the resources they need to succeed in their jobs. Keep them updated on any policy alterations that may have an impact on your clients.

Also, check the forms and other paperwork that clients are expected to complete to ensure they are as straightforward as possible, including sample completed forms and explicit instructions on how to achieve them.

If you and your employees are constantly asking, "How will what I am doing or intend to do affect my customers?" and take appropriate action based on the response to that question, you will have effectively established a customer service culture.

CHAPTER 9

The Crucial Steps to Exceptional Customer Service.

Excellent customer service is an important component of any business or professional contact. Providing a consumer with a fulfilling, enjoyable experience is often the difference between success and failure. While excellent customer service is easy to notice, performing as a professional is considerably more challenging.

As a manager, much of my understanding of customer service came from direct interaction with customers. As I began my first work out of college, I discovered that I was utilizing some of the talents I had gained previously, in addition to a few more strategies tailored to my position.

Many new professionals may lack early customer service experience from past positions. Lack of a fundamental grasp of excellent customer service can be detrimental to an individual's career in any field.

Comprehending a few fundamental principles can assist a new expert in ensuring that clients leave interactions delighted.

The first step toward providing exceptional customer service is establishing a personal connection. The importance of stating your name and inquiring how you may assist is important for creating the tone of the conversation.

Pay attention to how a waiter interacts with diners at any restaurant. They always take the time to greet the customer and build a cordial rapport. While this step may look trivial, it is the bedrock of any outstanding customer service engagement. Also, it assists in putting the customer at ease and makes you appear more approachable.

Also, it is important not to downplay the customer's difficulties. As a manager, I often receive questions that I have already answered; yet, I make every connection as personal as possible. While I may have dealt with a similar issue with another client, assuming my current customer is struggling with the same issue is dangerous. Each problem is unique and requires an individualized response.

Active listening is one approach to ensure that you offer personalized attention—even for the most commonplace issues.

Allowing the customer to express their problem or concern without interrupting them and restating their problem to ensure clarity are both approaches to promote active listening and excellent customer service.

While providing customer service, it's important to avoid assumptions about how well the consumer understands the situation. Troubleshooting with clients should always start with the basics and work its way up from there.

I have a set of straightforward questions that I ask every consumer who is having an issue. Covering these fundamentals, which can be as easy as reloading a webpage, ensures that all feasible resolutions have been exhausted before going on to more complex ones.

Any customer service encounter should strive to achieve the best possible degree of customer satisfaction. Going the extra mile to handle a problem or answer a question can have a significant influence. First, I focused entirely on fixing client problems, but as I progressed in my career, I realized it was important to make sure the issue didn't reoccur in the future.

Identifying the source of the problem or arming the client with the knowledge necessary to resolve it on their own adds a degree of service that makes the difference in a professional relationship.

Regrettably, there will be times when a customer's issue cannot be remedied over the phone or during a store visit. In some instances, an escalated reaction may be necessary to resolve the issue. Sending a product overnight, sending a technician, or issuing a refund are acceptable remedies for more serious difficulties.

When escalating a situation, it is important to provide a timeframe and ensure a response. Also, it is important to obtain all necessary information to ensure that the issue will be resolved without further contact with the customer; ensuring that your next interaction offers a solution is an aim!

Finally, there is no guarantee that the consumer will remain composed and collected during the chat. They may become irritated or aggressive if the answer you propose does not meet their requirements

Keeping a cool head and refraining from raising your voice when on the phone is important if this is the case. It's not uncommon for me to give the person in question a minute or two before bringing the problem to upper management.

Allowing a supervisor to address the issue demonstrates to the client that their concerns are significant and helps to alleviate tension during the talk. In extreme circumstances, such as when a client makes threats or engages in violent behavior, it is okay to request that the individual leave or discontinue the call, although this is an extreme response.

Providing excellent customer service is a talent that every professional can acquire. Most customer service transactions will conclude positively by focusing on tone, active listening, and providing outstanding service.

Because skill development takes time, do not be scared to try new ways or strategies. Only by experimenting with fresh ways can you develop as a professional and improve your customer service skills.

CHAPTER 10

Customer Service and Developing a Culture of High Performance.

Team Culture has a significant impact on our Customer Service Team's performance and the quality of service we provide to our Customers. The most important factor is TEAM CULTURE.

Our goal in Customer Service is for each of our Customers to receive superior Customer Service and an experience with our organization that exceeds their expectations on every call to our organization. Each caller will have a positive experience that will entice him or her to return and make additional purchases.

To accomplish this goal, we hire qualified candidates, train them well and compensate them fairly. Will this, therefore, ensure that this new Team Member can provide exceptional Customer Service in the future? Perhaps a more pertinent question is if the new Team Member will attempt to produce a successful conclusion for our customers and us.

Team Culture's Influence

This is a difficult question because the response is so individualized and dependant on the person answering it. It is much more dependent on the team's character in which they are placed - on the Culture of that particular group. Within a few days of instruction, the group will significantly impact this new individual's thinking.

They will speak about their role and customers to match. 'All these customers are idiots; they never listen properly.' 'Customers are constantly blaming us for things that are not our responsibility.' 'Our products are substandard, which is why our customers are constantly dissatisfied.'

Each of these phrases reflects a different culture of the team. Each Culture is recognized, and its members will behave predictably toward their

Customers - the Culture will dictate behavior. Each of the scenarios above illustrates how each group will respond in a manner that will certainly NOT result in an excellent Customer Service experience.

For instance, a team that believes they are the experts and are superior to these truly illiterate Customers will be harsh and impatient with their callers. They refuse to show off their skills in front of their clients and are unreceptive to instruction. Aggressive Team believes they are not the problem, but rather, it is the customers' fault!!!

The intriguing thing about Team Culture is how pervasive it is. New members rapidly come to believe that the Team's worldview is accurate and 'common sense.' Other casual statements made by Team Members quickly distinguish between the Submissive and Passive Aggressive Team Cultures.

They adopt the beliefs and attitudes that promote that specific Team Culture, which shapes the Team's behavioral norms - what is and is not acceptable behavior inside this group. If we wish to improve team performance, we must first change our BELIEFS.

A Successful Customer Service Team's Beliefs

A high-performing Customer Service Team possesses a distinct team culture dubbed the Assertive, Customer-Focused Culture. They have a set of attitudes, beliefs, and behavioral standards that ENSURES they perform extraordinarily well with their customers and drives them to grow consistently.

Remember that Team Culture is derived from the Team's shared ideals. We achieve this Assertive, Customer-Focused Culture by defining the desired beliefs and continuously fostering and supporting them inside our Team Culture.

It is feasible to change the culture of an organization or even a single team. We change the culture by attempting to change our beliefs.

The fundamental ideas are as follows:

1. This is a good organization worth working for; and

2. What we do as a business adds VALUE to our consumers. (Includes Exceeding Expectations)

3. We value our customers. External factors are essential. Internal customers are also customers

4. We are ALL a part of this company, united by a common goal.

5. As a team, we have a vital role to play in realizing our Shared Goal.

6. Our Team Shared Purpose's success depends on my work, and my efforts are valuable.

7. This Team has seven members, and each one of them is a part of it. It is each team member's responsibility to meet the Team Leader's standards. Customer expectations are managed and exceeded by everyone.

8. Success is desirable; success is desirable.

9. To succeed, we must continually improve - both individually and as a high-performing team.
We are a good team - and in a month or a year, we will be an even better team.

These beliefs are essential to Customer Service success. If you are a management team member, encourage your managers to improve one belief per month. If you are a Team Leader, follow the same procedure. Collaborate with the team on how we can improve each belief. You will quickly see the benefits in terms of increased performance, motivation, and job happiness.

CHAPTER 11

Overnight Improvement of Your Customer Service Skills.

Whatever method you utilize, it is crucial to track your customer service levels to increase client retention.

How can you quantify customer service?

Do you track it by the number of times they return to your establishment?

Do you quantify it by the number of referrals you receive?

Or do you gauge it by the postcards placed on each table to solicit client feedback?

Another thing you want is a consumer who is annoyed with your business's services. This type of consumer will tell nearly ten people about their negative experiences at your business.

However, if this same consumer had a fantastic time at your establishment, they may only tell about it to roughly three people. It's not much, but it's a lot better than informing ten people about the substandard service they received.

You've heard this phrase before, but it's still true: "Always Remember That the Customer Is Always Right."

Even though most of us did not adhere to the new "customer is always right" approach, I observed some coworkers taking it seriously. When I worked as a worker bee for a huge retailer, they emphasized this to everyone present. Regrettably, that phrase slipped their minds, and they continued to perform their duties as usual.

This is another illustration of how to treat your customers like gold. I used to work at this establishment where the boss instructed employees to "treat each customer as if they were a king." Believe it or not, this flew over my mind, but I carried on with the interview anyhow.

No, but honestly, you must have a robust customer service strategy that both you and your personnel can adhere to. This could include a greeting at the entrance. Simple policy modifications of this nature establish professionalism and give customers and clients the impression that you are someone who knows what you're doing.

When you consider it, this is not a far-fetched notion. Making consumers pleased benefits your business and increases referrals from existing customers. However, do not bother going there if you do not believe that a testimonial with some customer is worthwhile.

If you want repeat customers, emphasize customer service. Simple gestures such as how you speak to people and how you treat them will significantly impact them. I sincerely hope you're already utilizing these customer service practices in your organization.

Ken Blanchard, a management guru, expressed it best when he stated, "Historically, a leader was a boss. Today's leaders must collaborate with their followers; they can no longer rule exclusively based on positional authority."

Effective company practices begin at the top and trickle down. This rule also applies to solid customer service techniques. If management treats consumers with respect, employees will do the same.

Managers who show appreciation for staff by making themselves available to consumers will inspire those under their supervision to do the same. This comprehensive approach to great customer service benefits the entire organization and helps retain customers.

How can this technique be successfully adopted within an organization?

Visibility of Management

Management should be regarded as a team member.

Is this the perception that your employees and consumers have of your organization's management?

Do clients always have to contact the manager if they have a problem?

Isn't it preferable to have the manager out and about in the store, immediately visible and developing connections with customers on an equal footing with other employees?

When it comes to management visibility, perception is important.

Management Should Be Responsive.

Do staff feel comfortable approaching their bosses with suggestions for prospective customer service improvements?

If they do not believe they can, they may lose out on some suggestions that can help retain existing consumers and attract new ones. Management should be reachable by employees, but customers should also understand that management can assist them.

When a customer attempts to resolve a problem, one of the worst impressions that may be left is that management is frightening. Management should be a partner in resolving the issue as early as possible.

The top-down method may need management to receive refresher customer service training. It's necessary to be reminded periodically that the client is the most important component of any successful business operation.

Once management has established this concept in their corporate mindset, the customer service culture may truly thrive within an organization, reaping the benefits of increased customer connections and employee morale.

If you want to remain profitable and successful in business, you must adhere to these marketing fundamentals. You must follow a step-by-step method to bring customers into your establishment and convince them to buy from you again and again (and providing a referral would assist!).

CONCLUSION.

Managers must possess exceptional customer service abilities to meet the requirements of others properly. This goes beyond the call of duty to ensure that customers are satisfied with their purchases of products and services. One will discuss what may be done to facilitate this.

There are many areas that management can teach their personnel when they are regularly in contact with customers. Employees are expected to demonstrate consumer attentiveness.

As a result, they can relate and sympathize when necessary. This does not mean acting phony but rather acting authentically. Those who live in the United States as foreigners will notice and enjoy it.

Indeed, he or she will feel cherished as a result, which makes an effort worthwhile. Anyone who enters the business will notice this, and they will prefer to deal with the individual who cares about them rather than the person who does not.

Respect is a constant requirement. Businesses may instill this in their workers by demonstrating the correct way to interact with all consumers. For instance, one method to accomplish this is through manners.

They can arrange for a particular class or training session to facilitate this. Everyone is obliged to participate in role-playing exercises and pass the course before working with anybody else in the organization.

When a consumer inquires about an item, it is promptly delivered. Customer service entails going above and beyond what is requested of him or her at the time. This may include letting the individual try the item on before completing the purchase.
When someone acts in this manner, they demonstrate servant-leadership by prioritizing the needs of others over their own. The consumer is ecstatic.

Contrary to general belief, the customer is not always right. When a complaint is received, management has instructed the employee on how to handle it successfully. At times, this may entail a period of humility. The ability to succeed in this situation requires patience. Regardless, the goal is to satisfy all clients.

Customer service skills enable an individual to perform well in their career. The objective is to satisfy consumers regardless of whether they are correct or incorrect. All will succeed by developing patience, exceeding expectations, etiquette, respect, and sensitivity.

Best of Luck!

Management Skills for Managers

1. Time Management for Managers
2. Employee Coaching for Managers
3. Team Building for Managers
4. Self Confidence for Managers
5. Negotiation Skills for Managers
6. Customer Service Skills for Managers
7. Assertiveness for Managers

www.ingramcontent.com/pod-product-compliance
Lightning Source LLC
Chambersburg PA
CBHW070123230526
45472CB00004B/1396